Big Baa Dill

Written by Martin Waddell
Illustrated by Graham Philpot

Big Bad Bill wanted to rob the mill on the hill.
'Who lives in the mill on the hill?' asked Bill.

'Nobody lives there!' said the kids in the town.
'We never go there.
We are all scared of the mill on the hill.'

'I'm not scared!' said
Big Bad Bill.
'I'm a very brave burglar...'

and he set off to rob the mill on the hill.

Bill climbed the hill to the mill.

Nobody climbed it behind him.

Bill opened the gate with a C-R-E-A-K.

Nobody shut it behind him.

Bill looked through the window.
Nobody was there, so . . .

Bill climbed through the window into the mill.
Nobody climbed in behind him.

Bill went up the stairs.

Nobody went up behind him.

Bill got his bag
and filled it with swag.
Nobody watched him.

'I'm a very brave burglar!' said Big Bad Bill.
'I'm not scared of the mill on the hill.
I'm not scared of Nobody!'

Then . . .

Nobody went tap tap tap on the floor.
Big Bad Bill jumped.

Nobody switched the light on and . . .

Nobody switched the light off and . . .

on – off and . . .

on – off and . . .

on – off and . . .

Nobody bumped the swag on Bill's head.

Bill ran to the door but . . .

Nobody banged the door shut, and Nobody locked it. Bill couldn't get out.

Then . . .

Nobody banged on the ceiling
and . . .

Nobody bounced on the bed
and . . .

Nobody whistled in Big Bad Bill's ear and . . .

Nobody jumped on Big Bad Bill's toe and . . .

Nobody pulled Big Bad Bill's beard then . . .

Nobody threw the swag on the floor and pulled the swag bag over Big Bad Bill's head, and . . .

Nobody threw him out of the mill through the window.

Big Bad Bill ran down the hill
all covered in bag with no swag,
which made the kids laugh.

He never went back to Nobody's Mill
and he never will because
(although he's Big and Bad still)
he's scared of Nobody and
Nobody's not scared of Bill.